KEVIN'S BIG FE[AR]
Learn To Handle Emotions At School Like A Champ

By
Caleb Ellis

This book belongs to

_____

_____

Dedication Page

This book is lovingly dedicated to all the children who experience big emotions in school.

As a teacher and father, I've seen the challenges you face. I've witnessed how they can sometimes seem overwhelming. However, I want you to remember this: You are more powerful than your emotions. You have the strength to control them, to navigate every situation, and to handle school like a champ!

I've got tips to help you cope in school, when your emotions are hard to bare.

When you're feeling angry or sad, take deep breaths and count to ten.

Just pause and relax to calm yourself down, that helps me and my friends.

Use your words and talk it out,
instead of fighting, that works best.

If you need a break ask your teacher, that helps if you are getting stressed.

While at recess, if someone starts to tease you on the bleachers

If you get a bad score on your test, and you feel your emotions starting to climb.

I used to have a hard time in school.
I would get angry and break the rules.

I felt so alone and misunderstood,
my confidence was always low.

But once I learned to control my emotions, my confidence began to grow.

I'm glad I can share my story with you, and show what you can do too.

When you're feeling like you're losing control, there are things that you can do.

Embrace all differences,
Never discriminate.

Thanks for listening to me,
your future is mighty bright.

Remember breathe and count to 10, instead of anger and trying to fight.

Coping Resources

What does coping mean?

Coping - finding ways to make yourself feel better when you're feeling upset or having a hard time. It's like finding a way to help yourself feel happy again.

Example: If you are playing a card game with your friend and they beat you instead of getting upset and throwing cards, you can take a deep breath and say "good game." This is controlling your emotions and coping with the sadness of loosing the right way.

5 Strategies To Help You Cope In School

1. Deep Breathing: When things get tough, take a big, deep breath in through your nose, hold it for a second, then slowly let it out through your mouth. This can help you feel a little calmer.
2. Counting to Ten: If you feel like you're getting too upset or angry, try counting slowly to ten in your head. This can give you a little time to calm down.
3. Taking a Break: If things feel like they're too much, it's okay to take a little break. You could ask your teacher if you can step outside for a moment, or just close your eyes and imagine your favorite place.
4. Saying Kind Things to Yourself: Sometimes, when we're feeling upset or stressed, we can say mean things to ourselves in our head. Try to say nice things instead, like "I'm doing my best" or "I can handle this."
5. Talking to Someone: If you're feeling really upset or sad, find someone you trust, like a teacher or a friend, and tell them about it. Sometimes just talking about our problems can make them feel a little less big and scary.

Made in the USA
Middletown, DE
02 March 2024